SINGAPORE'S GIFT TO THE WORLD

Singapore 1893. One cool tropical morning, Miss Agnes Joaquim was tending to her garden when she came upon an unusual orchid bloom growing amidst a clump of bamboo. Coloured a delicate mauve, it was round and full, with a purple lip. A brand new hybrid, this was named Vanda Miss Joaquim. As the first natural hybrid of the island, it was chosen as Singapore's National Flower in 1981.

Today, everyone associates Singapore with its orchids. The wealth of free-flowering orchids that one sees in Singapore is the result of a single-mindedness of purpose and ingenuity of a few individuals plus a lot of hard work and patience, the recurring ingredients of the success stories of Singapore.

Such is the concept of Ms Joaquim Singapore, which takes its inspiration from our Singapore orchids, translating this into products of art and beauty that capture the very spirit of Singapore — lively...creative...contemporary.

We welcome you to Ms Joaquim Singapore curio shop. Here you will find her museum collection of prominent Singapore orchid hybrids, named after well-known visiting dignitaries and events of the world. All these translated into high quality merchandise, which includes the ubiquitous tropical orchid-designer Singapore Shirt and a collection by top Asian designers featuring the new Singapore Dress — an elegant wear created for those special occasions.

As you stroll through the quaint little shop, you will discover too her prized orchid collection of gift sets, beautiful collectibles, jewellery, household objects, stationery, poster prints and local foodstuffs. And even a book on the cherished Vanda Miss Joaquim, entitled *A Joy Forever*.

You'll find shopping at Ms Joaquim an experience not to be missed. What better way to take a piece from Ms Joaquim as Singapore's gift to the world.

Ms Joaquim Singapore Boutique • Millenia Walk #01-48/49 • SINGAPORE • Tel: 3374778 • www.msjoaquim.com.sg

A THING OF BEAUTY IS A JOY FOR EVER
ITS LOVELINESS INCREASES; IT WILL NEVER
PASS INTO NOTHINGNESS; BUT STILL WILL KEEP
A BOWER QUIET FOR US, AND A SLEEP
FULL OF SWEET DREAMS, AND HEALTH,
AND QUIET BREATHING.
—

from *Endymion*, John Keats

A Joy Forever

VANDA MISS JOAQUIM

SINGAPORE'S NATIONAL FLOWER

—

TEOH ENG SOON

Times Editions

A JOY FOREVER

© 1982 Times Books International
Revised edition 1998
Published by Times Editions
an imprint of Times Editions Pte Ltd
Times Centre
1 New Industrial Road
Singapore 536196
Tel: (65) 2848844 Fax: (65) 2854871
Email: te@corp.tpl.com.sg

Online Bookstore:
http://www.timesone.com.sg/te

Water colour paintings courtesy of
the Singapore Botanic Gardens:

Pg 32 HB No. 24(a), *Vanda x Agnes Joaquim*
by James D'Alwis, May 1893;

Pg 47 HB No. 4, *Aerides rosea: Langkawi*
by James D'Alwis, June 1890;

Pg 62 (left) HB No. 34 *Vanda purpurea x Joaquim no. 3*
by Juraimi, August 1948;

Pg 62 (middle) HB No. 38 *Vanda teres x tricolor var.
purpurea* by Juraimi, 1949.

Text and photographs by Dr Teoh Eng Soon

Designed by Tuck Loong

Scanning of photographs by
Superskill Graphics Pte Ltd

Colour separation by
United Graphic Pte Ltd

Printed in Singapore

ISBN 981 204 966 5

Contents

Preface

In picking Vanda Miss Joaquim as the national flower, Singapore has gained the unique distinction of being the only nation to have a hybrid as its national flower. At the same time the flower has an original distribution confined to Singapore's boundaries, which, given the size of the island, is indeed remarkable.

Most countries and states are forced to settle for flowers whose distribution extends beyond their national boundaries. For example, Costa Rica's Flor de San Sebastian (*Cattleya skinneri*) was first discovered in Guatemala and is widely distributed throughout Central America, while Guatemala's Monja Blanca (*Lycaste virginalis*) is found in Mexico, El Salvador and Honduras, Minnesota's Moccasin Orchid (*Cypripedium reginae*) occurs in China, and Queensland's famous Cooktown Orchid (*Dendrobium phalaenopsis*) is also native to Indonesian Larat and Papua New Guinea. Miraculously, the single plant discovered by Agnes Joaquim in her garden at Tanjong Pagar in 1893 has truly been bountiful, and has multiplied into millions of plants. It rapidly became established as a popular garden plant in Singapore, then throughout South-east Asia at the turn of the century, and later it flourished in Hawaii, Florida, tropical America and Sri Lanka.

Before the Second World War, Vanda Miss Joaquim was the most popular orchid in Singapore. Nearly every garden had a few beds devoted to it. It has fallen into neglect during the last twenty years because commercial growers have concentrated on raising scorpion orchids. As a result, it is now more widely grown and better utilised in Hawaii, but within a few years this charming *Vanda* should become a familiar sight in Singapore again. It is a tough, hardy plant which is extremely easy to propagate. When grown to a man's height and exposed to full sun, massed plantings of this orchid provide solid banks of delicate mauve all year round. Since it is a splendid flower for landscaping it has helped fulfil our then Prime Minister Lee Kuan Yew's call "to make Singapore a green, shady city filled with fruits and flowers by the 1990s".

The choice of an orchid as Singapore's national flower is most appropriate because orchids have long been identified with Singapore. No orchid is more worthy than Agnes Joaquim's flower. It was the first hybrid from Singapore. In fact it was the first hybrid *Vanda* to be registered. For ease of cultivation and productivity it has

no rival. It is so free-flowering that it has served as a yardstick for orchid hybridisers. One story goes that one of the Rothschildes paid 500 guineas for a cutting of the original plant during the 19th century, but nowadays Vanda Miss Joaquim is found in such abundance that it is no longer an expensive plant to buy or own.

There are now hundreds of colourful, beautiful, gorgeous orchids in Singapore, several undoubtedly more lovely than the Vanda Miss Joaquim. Hybrids continue to improve and there will always be newer, more beautiful orchids.

But the beginning was Vanda Miss Joaquim.

Note: Some photographs of old hybrids have been removed to make way for recent arrivals. The data has been updated by the inclusion of a few paragraphs, identifiable by their bracketing. —TES (3/18/98)

Opposite: "The Singapore raised hybrid Vanda Miss Joaquim is probably for us the best orchid in the world." *Malayan Orchid Review*, March 1931.

Vanda Miss Joaquim

and Other Contenders

Vanda Miss Joaquim has been known by various names: Vanda Joaquim, the "Wah-Kim" orchid, Vanda Agnes Joaquim, and the Princess Aloha Orchid. On April 15, 1981, it became the national flower of Singapore following an announcement by then Minister for Culture S. Dhanabalan.

Its proper name is Vanda Miss Joaquim, the national flower being the variety Agnes.

According to the Minister for Culture the designation of a national flower was "part of an overall effort to foster national pride and identity". After years of deliberation, a national committee comprising representatives from the Ministry of Culture, the Parks and Recreation Department, the Singapore Tourist Promotion Board, the Singapore Institute of Standards and Industrial Research and the Orchid Society of South-east Asia chose Vanda Miss Joaquim from amongst 40 contenders, including some 30 orchids, "because of its resilience and year-round blooming quality".

This did not come as a surprise. A tour of the Singapore Botanic Gardens will show that many of the flowering shrubs are not indigenous. Malaysia had already chosen the beautiful hibiscus as its national flower, while the Philippines selected the fragrant jasmine, **Sampaguita** (*Jasminum sambac*). The Thai national flower is the yellow cassia. In this part of the world, Singapore has been the trendsetter in orchids for nearly a century and it hosted the Fourth World

Orchid Conference in 1963. What was more logical than to choose an orchid as its national flower?

THE ORCHID IN ORIENTAL CULTURE

The admiration for orchids goes back a long way in oriental cultural heritage. The word "Vanda" is derived from a Sanskrit word referring to *Vanda roxburghii* and other epiphytes. Two orchids (*Dendrobium moniliforme* and *Bletilla hyacinthina*) have the honour of being included in the *Materia Medica* of the mythical Chinese Emperor, Shen Nung (28th century B.C.) who is credited with the invention of agriculture and medicine. The orchid was also mentioned in the ancient Chinese classics, such as *The Book of Poetry* (1000–600 B.C.). The orchid referred to was probably the "tassel grass" (*Spiranthes sinensis*). Confucius (circa 551–479 B.C.) compared the company of good friends with a room full of fragrant orchids. The **lan hua** *Cymbidium viridescens* and *Cymbidium ensifolium* were probably the first orchids to be domesticated and they featured prominently in Chinese painting and literature. In Chinese culture, the orchid is the symbol of the scholar: unassuming, simple in its needs, plebeian and yet endowed with charm and subtle elegance.

Opposite: Vanda Miss Joaquim flowering on new propagations.

Top right: Spring Orchid by Cheng Ssu-hsiao (1250–1300) Album leaf; ink on paper (Courtesy of the Osaka Municipal Museum). There is a similar painting in the Smithsonian Institution Freer Gallery of Art.

It grows in isolated clumps on barren rocks; unattended it survives even in a harsh environment. Confucius said:

> The tse-lan grows in the valleys
> and does not withhold its fragrance
> even though it is not appreciated by man.

The orchid has also been used to symbolise people. In the Osaka Municipal Museum there is a famous painting of uprooted orchids from the Yuan Dynasty, one of the dark periods in Chinese history. It was painted by Cheng Ssu-hsiao (1250–1300) who employed the concept of uprooted orchids to depict the plight of the displaced nation. His inscription on the painting reads:

> I have been asking Hsi-huang (the ancient hermit)
>   with my head bowed:
> Who are you—and why did you come to this land?
> I opened my nostrils before making the painting.
> And there, floating everywhere in the sky, is the antique
>   fragrance undying.

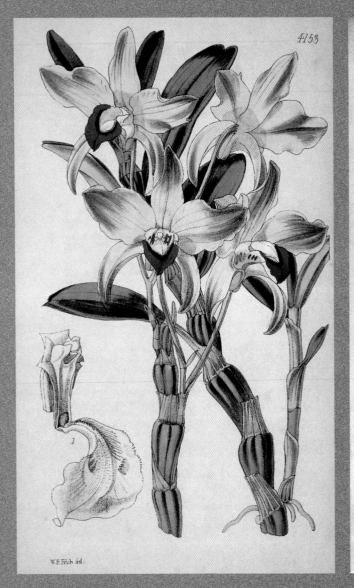

W.E. Fitch del.

Syd^m Edwards Del.   F. Sansom Sc.   Pub. by S. Curtis. Walworth. Sep^t 1. 1812.

Likewise, Japan, which has imbibed much of Chinese culture from the Tang to the Sung Dynasty, has been enamoured with the **Ran** for many centuries. In feudal Japan, Ran referred to 200 varieties of *Cymbidium* which were distinguished not by their flowers but by the patterns of their leaves; and to the stone orchid (*Dendrobium moniliforme*) and the wind orchid (*Neofinetia falcata*) which were native to Japan. These orchids had two things in common: the flowers were not striking, though they had a delicate, penetrating fragrance; and their foliage was beautiful.

During the Tokugawa Period (1603–1867) the Shogun grew orchids and spent much time admiring the plants. The samurai were generally known to favour the **Fu Ran** or "wind orchid". Some of the feudal lords became so fond of their orchids that they carried their plants with them wherever they went. To keep the orchids in sight they were suspended from the ceiling of their palanquins. Royal peers preferred the stone orchid and perfumed their clothes with its flowers. The flowers were also worn by ladies of the court in the belief that they would ward off illness. In a famous

Opposite left: In medieval Europe orchid tubers were consumed as aphrodisiacs which they really were not. How different the ancient Chinese practice, dating back to 2500 B.C. which valued the "stone orchid", *Dendrobium moniliforme* for its alleged ability to reduce fever, stimulate appetite, restore strength and prolong life. The orchid grows on rocks and trees in Korea, Japan and Taiwan.

Opposite right: Since 2600 B.C the white matted, fleshy tubers of the lovely *Bletilla hyacinthina*, the "white chicken", were boiled to make a drink which cured epistaxis and internal bleeding. They are also used in the manufacture of porcelain.

orchid manual written by Joan Matsuoko by imperial command in 1728, the author summarised the instructions for growing *Cymbidium* in only twelve characters:

> In spring do not put them outdoors,
> In summer, not too much sun,
> In autumn, not too dry,
> In winter, not too wet.

MYTHICAL ORIGINS

In the South-east Asian region, orchids have been featured in folklore and several species were held in high regard. In the dim recesses of virgin forest, hidden from the eyes of ordinary men the jewel orchid, *Macodes petola*, can be found. It grows on moss-covered rocks bathed by small streams. Its velvety heart-shaped leaves are a delicate blend of cinnamon, purple, olive and moss green, the colours changing with the play of the tremulous light. According to a Javanese legend, the jewel orchid sprouted from shreds of a shimmering magical scarf left on a jagged rock by a gracious goddess. In Sumatra, the flowers of the black orchid (*Coelogyne pandurata*), were used to bless crops, and in Malaysia, *Cymbidium finlaysonianum* was worn as a talisman to ward off evil spirits. And such was the alleged mystical power of the white pigeon orchid (*Dendrobium crumenatum*) that up until 1930 it was used in Kuala Kangsar, Malaysia, to counter 'bewitchment'. The plant was used to sprinkle water through the house

5084

Above: Black orchid.

after a death had occurred to keep the deceased's spirit from haunting the premises. In some Indonesian islands, a century ago, only princesses were permitted to sport the moon orchid, **anggrek bulan** (*Phalaenopsis amabilis*) in their hair.

A WORTHY CHOICE

Though it is not ensconced in any myth or legend, no orchid is more worthy of being Singapore's national flower than the Vanda Miss Joaquim. It is the oldest and the sole indigenous natural hybrid. Like many Singaporeans, its ancestral roots are foreign, yet it is totally at home in Singapore, adapted to the equatorial lowland climate. While other flowers languish in the midday sun, Vanda Miss Joaquim is invigorated by the humidity, heat and brilliant sunshine. In fact, under such conditions, it flowers continuously throughout the year. For nearly 70 years it reigned supreme in the tropical lowlands.

The clone discovered by Agnes Joaquim in her garden in 1893 proliferated into millions of plants and was, at one time, cultivated by the hundreds of acres. During the Second World War, when some Pacific nations were bent on destruction, Vanda Miss Joaquim transcended the mood of the period and came to evoke love. American soldiers on furlough in the Hawaiian Islands, enchanted by the beauty of the Singapore flower, mailed thousands of blooms home to their loved ones. It was an auspicious prelude to the blossoming of the orchid industry after the War.

Above: (top) Jewel orchid; *(bottom):* White pigeon orchid.

Right: In some of the Indonesian islands where they were known as the **anggrek bulan** or "Flowers of the Moon", the lovely white *phalaenopsis* were worn on the hair by princesses as a mark of their royalty. It is one of the most popular orchids in the world today and very much hybridised.

Today everyone associates Singapore with orchids. Singapore's orchid flower export amounted to $15 million in 1979. (To promote this industry, the Singapore Trade Development Board organised the IOSS 93 (International Orchid Show, Singapore 1993) which attracted 1,500 participants and displays from ASEAN, USA, United Kingdom, Australia, New Zealand, Japan and China. Orchid exports in 1994 amounted to $25 million, with the lion's share going to Japan.)

In hotels, offices and homes orchids are commonly found in abundance. Orchids preserved in gold by RISIS are worn as jewellery. The currency and postage stamps feature orchids. Perhaps it may come as a surprise to some people that most of Singapore's native orchid species have insignificant, evanescent flowers (the exception being the giant orchid *Grammatophyllum speciosum*, which is extremely rare). The wealth of free-flowering orchids one sees in Singapore is not a gift of nature but the result of the single-minded purpose of a few men and a lot of hard work and patience, the recurring ingredients of the success stories of Singapore.

Left: The white pigeon orchid, *Dendrobium crumenatum*, is probably the commonest orchid species in Singapore, being abundant on roadside trees even in the heart of the city. Its fragrant flowers make a sudden spectacular appearance exactly nine days after a thunderstorm but by evening they have all faded.

Opposite: A strong contender for the role of national flower, the native white scorpion orchid, *Arachnis hookerana*, is the important stud that produced all the long-lasting scorpion orchids which are exported worldwide.

HYBRIDISATION

Eric Holttum, who was to do pioneering work on orchid hybridisation in Singapore, came out in 1922, fresh from Kew and Cambridge. After observing the Vanda Miss Joaquim in her full glory, he concluded that "the sun of the species orchid is setting . . . Reasonably enough, the hybrid outshines its ancestors. The orchid goes or has gone the way of the rose, the dahlia, the sweet pea; in short, all cultivated flowers. Man improves on nature."

In 1928, Eric Holttum and John Laycock, a lawyer by profession, initiated a hybridisation programme at the Singapore Botanic Gardens which was to have a profound effect on orchid growing in the tropics. At the same time they formed the Malayan Orchid Society (now renamed the Orchid Society of Southeast Asia) to stimulate a wider interest in orchids. Together, Holttum and Laycock raised a string of hybrids which were, in most cases, more free-flowering than their parents. However, none could surpass Vanda Miss Joaquim. The names of these early hybrids are now a part of local orchid history and although 50 years have passed, some are still being cultivated as cut flowers for export—Aranda Deborah, Arachnis Maggie Oei, Aranthera Mohamed Haniff, Aranthera James Storie and Oncidium Golden Shower.

Opposite: Code-named SBG770, Vanda Tan Chay Yan has won the hearts of orchid growers all over the world with its bold flowers the colour of a tropical sunset. Its appearance in 1952 has been described as the strongest stimulus to orchid breeding in Singapore and Malaysia after the War.

After the War, new studs were introduced and more gardeners tried their hand at breeding orchids. Bigger, brighter, better flowers in a vast array of shapes and colours made their entry into the Singapore orchid world. Prominent among these new hybrids were Vanda Tan Chay Yan, Vanda Tan Chin Tuan, Aranda Wendy Scott, Aranthera Beatrice Ng and much later on, Aranda Noorah Alsagoff. Aranda Christine, imported from Penang, became the most cultivated orchid in Singapore during the 1970s.

Most of these hybrids were included among some 30 orchids placed before the selection committee for the national flower but from a historical perspective, Vanda Miss Joaquim was a clear winner over the competition. Some of the more beautiful orchids had negative attributes, such as uncertainty of parentage, a loss of precedence to other countries in the registration of its hybrid name, or simply membership to an alien genus. Even in 1957, when the orchid world and the members of the Malayan Orchid Society were smitten by the beauty of the new Vanda Tan Chay Yan, the Malayan Orchid Society chose Vanda Miss Joaquim for its crest. Today, Vanda Tan Chay Yan has been surpassed by many hybrids.

One major contender for the national flower was the white scorpion orchid (*Arachnis hookerana*). It is the important parent or grandparent of nearly all the scorpion orchids that form the backbone of Singapore's orchid trade, passing on to them a tremendous toughness, the ability to

withstand full sunlight or torrential rains, and flori-ferousness in a lowland, tropical climate. The white scorpion orchid is native to Singapore but it has a distribution that extends along the coastal fringes of the Malay Peninsula on its eastern seaboard through Singapore and the Rhio islands to Borneo. It has been collected from Punggol and Pulau Seletar and, according to George Alphonso, who did a lot of collecting for the Singapore Botanic Gardens, perhaps it still grows wild on Pulau Senang. At one time it was found in great abundance in open country. It takes an orchid scientist to admire this flower for its own sake today (whatever it may do for its hybrids); to many, it is a pale, ungainly, masculine flower. Because of this and the fact that it flowers only twice a year, the white scorpion orchid was dropped from contention.

VANDA MISS JOAQUIM AND HER PARENTS

As mentioned earlier, the original Vanda Miss Joaquim was a natural hybrid between *Vanda hookerana* and *Vanda teres*. The correctness of its parentage has been proven by several repeat crossings between the two parent species. Every time the crossings were performed, whether in

Left: A recent member in a long line of hybrids between the scorpion orchids and Vanda, the Aranda Baby Teoh characterises the new trend in hybridising—large flowers, clear hues and a vase life of three weeks or more.

Opposite: Vanda Tan Chin Tuan is similar to Vanda Tan Chay Yan but is coloured a blue-mauve, a breakthrough in the 1950s with this type of flower. The colouration comes from its famous parent, Vanda Rothschildiana.

Singapore, Malaysia, Indonesia or Hawaii, the result was a flower similar (though not identical) to the original Vanda Miss Joaquim.

Vanda hookerana grows among low shrubs and thickets in swamps in Malaysia, peninsular Thailand, Sumatra and Borneo, sometimes with its roots and up to 30 cm of its stem submerged in water. It is the only orchid known to do this because ordinarily orchid roots cannot stand being waterlogged. At one time it was so common in Perak that it earned the name "Kinta weed". The flower of *Vanda hookerana* is distinguished by an immense purple lip which is spotted with blotches of dark purple, a delightful trait which it has passed on to Vanda Miss Joaquim. *Vanda hookerana* occurs in two forms, the typical form with flowers of light mauve accentuated by the spotted purple lip, and a rare albino variety. One to four flowers open simultaneously on a spray.

The other parent, *Vanda teres*, has a distribution extending from the foothills of the Himalayas to Burma, Thailand and Laos. It occurs in several forms: (1) variety Andersoni, which has a yellow serpentine lip, (2) variety

---

Left: Vanda hookerana. This once ubiquitous "weed" of the Kinta Valley is the orchid version of the sacred lotus; growing in mud it scrambles up thickets and bushes to hold its immaculate flowers to the sun. One Malaysian orchidophile told of dredgemasters seeing a vast sea "Kinta weeds" which they had to clear to get at the tin ore.

Opposite: Vanda teres is a parent of Vanda Miss Joaquim. It grows in full sunlight in the valleys and lowlands of Thailand, Laos, Burma and Bangladesh, but is shy blooming in Singapore.

aurorea, which has a strong magenta blush on the petals, (3) variety alba (or Candida) and (4) variety gigantea. In its native habitat it is found climbing tall tree trunks or in thickets, often branching until it becomes a large, tangled clump. The flowering season extends from April to July.

Vanda teres was discovered by N. Wallich in Sylhet (in what is now Bangladesh) and was introduced into cultivation in England in 1829. This was the period of the orchidomania in Europe. England was then the hub of the orchid-growing world. The plant did not flower till several years later. It was described by John Lindley in 1833. There was a gap of 23 years before *Vanda hookerana* was described

by H.G. Reichenbach in 1856. The first living specimen of *Vanda hookerana* was sent from Labuan to the firm of Veitch and Sons in England in 1879. That a natural hybrid should appear in Singapore only 14 years later in 1893 is indeed quite remarkable.

It is not known which of the varieties of *Vanda teres* had been accidentally pollinated by *Vanda hookerana* to produce the original Vanda Miss Joaquim (or whether it was a reverse cross which produced the hybrid). In any case, the resulting flower is intermediate between the two parents. A strong inflorescence of Vanda Miss Joaquim may carry up to 12 buds, usually with four flowers open at a time. Each flower is 5 cm across and 6 cm tall, and as is the case with its parents, the petals are twisted around so that the back surface faces front. The two petals and the dorsal (top) sepal are rosy-violet, and the lateral sepals are a pale mauve. The lip is very large and broad and the middle lobe extends out like a fan. It is coloured violet-rose, merging into a contrasting fiery orange at the centre. Over the orange patch, the lip is finely spotted with dark purple. Ridley, who first described the flower, summed up by saying: "it seems to have taken the form of *Vanda hookerana* and the colouring of *Vanda teres*".

The first repeat cross between *Vanda teres* var. aurorea and *Vanda hookerana* var. alba was made by John Laycock in 1928 in the hope that he might obtain a white Joaquim. It produced a mauve flower which was broader sideways.

Holttum named it var. Josephine after a grandniece of Agnes Joaquim. The second repeat cross was made by Chevalier in Bandoeng, Indonesia in 1937 and repeated at the Singapore Botanic Gardens in 1939. *Vanda teres* var. alba was pollinated by *Vanda hookerana*. The resultant hybrid, Vanda Miss Joaquim var. Rose Marie had larger flowers with overlapping segments of a delicate pale mauve, but it was not as free-flowering as the original Joaquim.

The only white Vanda Miss Joaquim (var. John Laycock) was finally bred by Yeoh Bok Choon of Johore in 1962 using two albino parents. It is still quite rare and the common white flower that looks like a white Joaquim is, in fact, a different hybrid called Vanda Poepoe var. Diana.

In Hawaii, Vanda Miss Joaquim has been repeatedly self-pollinated. Some of the seedlings produced exceedingly large flowers. Upon investigation, these plants were shown to contain twice the amount of DNA; they were tetraploid plants, the dream of every hybridiser. Tetraploid clones of Vanda Miss Joaquim have all been given varietal names such as Atherton, Douglas, Juliet, Hula Girl and Woodlawn. Many fine hybrids have been bred from these tetraploid forms of Vanda Miss Joaquim.

In spite of all the attempts to improve on the original Vanda Miss Joaquim, it was the natural hybrid alone which shot to fame. But Miss Joaquim's orchid had become so common that no one thought it necessary to give it a varietal name. Holttum has proposed that it be called variety Agnes. Insofar as it is now the national flower of Singapore, this specific clone should henceforth be designated variety Agnes.

Top left: Vanda Miss Joaquim var. Josephine is the result of a cross made by John Laycock between *Vanda teres* var. aurorea and the white form of *Vanda hookerana*. It was named in 1933 for the youngest daughter of the Joaquim family living in Kuala Lumpur. The variety Josephine is free-flowering and has more of the influence of *Vanda teres* in its shape.

Opposite: Raised in 1937 by C.A. Chevalier in Bandoeng, Java, Vanda Miss Joaquim variety Rose Marie is a cross between the white variety of *Vanda teres* and the common variety of *Vanda hookerana*. It flowered in 1945 but did not prove to be as floriferous as the variety Agnes and it had to reach a height of 1.5 metres before it would bloom.

Historical Background

$\mathcal{I}$n a more gentle time, before the War, when children still played in the streets and life ambled at a leisurely pace, ladies and even grown-up men found time for gardening. Nearly every front garden in Singapore had its hedge of Vanda Miss Joaquim whose crown of mauve blossoms decked the city with splashes of colour, up one street and down the next.

During the first half of this century the power of Miss Joaquim's orchid extended far beyond Singapore. It was the prima donna and was treated as the prized plant in private gardens in Malaya, Thailand, the Philippines, Ceylon, Hawaii, Florida and Central America. On looking back, it comes as a surprise that so many people could grow the plant without making a determined effort to learn something about the lady who discovered it, like using light bulbs and not knowing the name Edison.

WHO WAS AGNES JOAQUIM?

Until recently, the identity of the lady who discovered the flower had eluded us; in fact we have still been unable to obtain a photograph of her. Before the national flower was named, there were only two scraps of information about her. Henry Ridley in 1893 described her as "a lady residing in Singapore well known for her success as a horticulturist" and John Laycock in 1949 said that "she lived with her brother who practised law". Six blind men could tell us more about an elephant. A trace on her identity was initiated by the Straits Times Press in April 1981 when her *Vanda* became the national flower. Thanks to the fine efforts of their reporters and the assistance of 70-year-old Arshak Galstaun who is president of the Armenian Church in Singapore, contact was finally made with Basil Johannes, 88, a nephew of Agnes Joaquim. As far as we know, he is the only living person to have met her.

Agnes was the eldest daughter of Basil (alias Barsigh or Parsick) Joaquim and Urelia Zachariah who had a large family of 12 children. They were Armenians and belonged to the oldest Christian Church in Singapore, the Armenian Church which even had its fronting road named after it. Although the Armenians were a small community in Singapore they played an important role in its commerce. Basil was a diamond merchant and owned a large house with extensive grounds at 2 Narcis Street, off Tanjong Pagar Road ("Near Keppel Harbour," Saheb told Holttum. Saheb had been a foreman under Ridley in the Botanic Gardens.) Isaiah Zachariah, the father of Urelia, was a warden of Singapore's early Armenian community and one of the first members of Singapore's International Chamber of Commerce. Urelia was born in Singapore in 1828. She married Basil in 1852.

Agnes was born on April 7, 1854, the second child in the family. Her Armenian name was Ashghen, which had been the name of her maternal grandmother. Her brothers, Joe, Seth and Robert, grew up to be eminent barristers and Joe co-founded the legal firm called Braddel Brothers. Another brother, Arathoon, was Deputy Registrar of the Hackney Carriage Department.

Agnes was a gentle lady who loved gardening and church work. She was very close to her sister Regina, who was seven years her junior. According to Basil Johannes, his mother, Regina, and Agnes were "so alike in appearance they could have been twins". They spent a lot of time in the garden tending to the clumps of *Vanda hookerana* which had been collected from the mines in Perak, and *Vanda teres* which had come with a shipment of assorted orchids from Burma. Free-flowering shrubs were scarce in those days; with the even weather, a monotonous green would

Above: Regina Joaquim with her husband. This is the closest we have come to a picture of Agnes Joaquim; "Regina and Agnes were so alike they could have been twins." (Courtesy of Arshak Galstaun)

Opposite: "The beginning was Vanda Miss Joaquim."

pervade one's garden unless one had some bougainvillaea, crotons and a small collection of orchids. *Vanda hookerana* stood out because it flowered so freely, and during a good season it could put up a fine show of pink flowers, each individually accentuated by a large patch of purple. If not who would grow this straggly plant that looked so much like a weed!

Vanda teres was not as floriferous as *hookerana* but it had a fuller shape, better colour and flowered gregariously when it chose to do so, the flowers lasting for several weeks. A devoted gardener could always hope that the next flowering would be more splendid than the last. In this respect, it differed from the other orchids imported from Burma, such as the dendrobiums, which flowered only once after the dry season, and never again afterwards.

One morning while Agnes was loitering alone in the garden she came upon a new orchid flower nestled in a clump of bamboo. It was round and full, of a delicate mauve like the *Vanda teres* but it was flowering out of season. It had a large purple lip, though this was not quite as large or as dark as the lip of *Vanda hookerana*. Perhaps it was a new species! Agnes could not contain her excitement. Straightaway she took it to the Director of the Singapore Botanic Gardens. He confirmed that it was indeed a new orchid, unknown to science, a hybrid between *Vanda hookerana* and *Vanda teres*. The year was 1893 and Agnes was 39.

The Director of the Botanic Gardens was the brilliant Henry Ridley. "Mad Ridley" he was called, because he went about saying that the sap from some strange Brazilian tree could be made into all sorts of objects and held great economic promise for Malaya. He planted the first rubber trees in Singapore and Malaya, and initiated Malaysians into the rubber industry. Among his many side interests was orchids. Before coming to Singapore he had already published numerous papers on orchids. During his tenure as Director of the Gardens he collected material for a flora of Malaya and wrote *Malayan Orchids* which was published as a long article by the Proceedings of the Linnean Society of London.

Six years after discovering her orchid, Agnes Joaquim died, aged 45. She probably did not live long enough to know that she had discovered an ever-blooming wonder which was to influence orchid growing throughout the tropical regions of the world. She was buried at the Bukit Timah Cemetery behind the Istana. When this was converted into a park a few years ago, her tombstone together with those of her parents and her barrister brothers was removed to the Armenian Church where it now rests. Her epitaph contains the line:

"Let her own works praise her."

VANDA MISS JOAQUIM— NATURAL OR ARTIFICIAL HYBRID?

When Ridley announced the orchid in the Gardener's Chronicle of June 24, 1893, he stated that Agnes Joaquim "succeeded in crossing *Vanda hookerana* Rehb.f. and *Vanda teres*, two plants cultivated in almost every garden in Singapore". Nearly every orchidist since that time believed

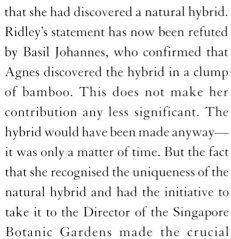

that she had discovered a natural hybrid. Ridley's statement has now been refuted by Basil Johannes, who confirmed that Agnes discovered the hybrid in a clump of bamboo. This does not make her contribution any less significant. The hybrid would have been made anyway— it was only a matter of time. But the fact that she recognised the uniqueness of the natural hybrid and had the initiative to take it to the Director of the Singapore Botanic Gardens made the crucial difference to orchid growing in the tropics.

Artificial hybridisation commenced in Singapore in 1928 following a visit by Hans Burgeff who taught Eric Holttum the method of asymbiotic culture whereby

Above: This drawing from the Herbarium of the Singapore Botanic Gardens has a date marked May 1893, probably referring to the date of the appearance of the national flower. (Courtesy of the Director, Singapore Botanic Gardens.)

Opposite: ". . . now, the national flower of Singapore, Vanda Miss Joaquim, variety Agnes."

orchids could be germinated in the laboratory. Orchid seeds do not contain any food stores and in nature they cannot germinate successfully unless they are first infected by a special fungus which provides them with sugar. The raising of orchid seedlings by the "natural method" was a closely guarded secret, known only to a handful of nurseries in England. The principles behind the method, i.e. the requirement of fungus, was not unravelled until 1899 when the French botanist Noel Barnard, wandering in the forest, beheld orchid seedlings and fungus growing in symbiosis on the forest floor. In 1921, an American scientist at Cornell, Lewis Knudson, developed a sterile culture medium containing glucose, mineral nutrients and agar on which orchid seeds could germinate and grow.

Natural hybrids are distinctly uncommon because, as a rule, an insect pollinator is faithful to its particular orchid species. However, capricious behaviour in insects cannot be completely ruled out. In Europe, swarms of natural hybrids have been found between closely related terrestrial orchid species, and natural hybrids also occur in *Dendrobium* orchids in Papua New Guinea. In the Malay Archipelago, several natural hybrids have been discovered from moth orchids. The insect which pollinates *Vanda hookerana* and Vanda Miss Joaquim is the carpenter bee (*Xylocopa sp.*) which is also known to be a pollinator of the white moth orchid (*Phalaenopsis amabilis*) and other flowers such as the Straits

Rhododendron; altogether, a most indiscriminate pollinator.

In 1940, J.A. la Doux of Kota Tinggi presented to the Singapore Botanic Gardens an unusual seedling of Vanda Miss Joaquim which he had found growing on a tree in his garden where he had long raised Vanda Miss Joaquim. Holttum commented that it was practically certain that this seedling arose from a self-pollinated flower of Vanda Miss Joaquim. Another natural hybrid formed from *Vanda hookerana*, Vanda Cooperi, was discovered in the garden of C.B. Cooper in Johore Bahru, just across the Straits from Singapore, nine years earlier. Mr Cooper grew all the three terete *Vanda* in his garden—*Vanda hookerana*, *Vanda teres* and Vanda Miss Joaquim. His hybrid was a cross between *Vanda hookerana* and Vanda Miss Joaquim.

The discovery of these hybrids lends additional support to the view that Vanda Miss Joaquim was indeed a natural hybrid.

THE CAREER OF VANDA MISS JOAQUIM

Henry Ridley always recognised a good thing when he saw it. A plant that flowered continuously while it multiplied by sending offshoots in all directions was simply unbelievable. Derived from the stock of *Vanda hookerana* which normally had its roots submerged in mud and water, Vanda Miss Joaquim could also be treated as a ground plant and it became extremely lush when heavily fertilised.

Opposite: ". . . chosen for its resilience and year-round blooming quality."

By dividing the plants very frequently, Ridley was able to produce a sizeable stock and within a few years he was distributing it to growers in Singapore. Throughout the length and breadth of Malaya and Singapore, Vanda Miss Joaquim became the favourite plant of every gardener who had any desire at all to grow flowering plants. The first issue of the *Malayan Orchid Review*, published in March 1931, eulogised the orchid in these words:

> The Singapore-raised hybrid, Vanda Miss Joaquim, is probably for us the best orchid in the world. What orchid can equal it for size, beauty of shape, beauty of colour, freedom of propagation and floribundity, taken all together? Where can one see anywhere in the world, solid banks and hedges of beautiful flowers to compare with this orchid in the gardens of Singapore?

A plant with such qualities, of course, did not come cheaply. In the 1920s, when it was still a rarity, one had to pay $5 per foot for a cutting. But Joaquim multiplied so rapidly that by 1931 the price had dropped to "$2 a clump of ten plants in flower or about to flower (about 4 to 5 feet high)". By comparison, the white scorpion orchid which grew wild in Malaya was selling at $1.50 for a clump of ten large plants, and other local species, such as *Spathoglottis plicata,* which could be collected from dry open areas of Singapore, and *Arundina graminifolia,* which was abundant in the hill stations of Malaya, were selling at a dollar per pot. Another ten years later, Vanda Miss Joaquim was selling at 50 cents for ten plants in a pot. Cultivation of the

Above: Arundina graminifolia. This showy orchid used to be a familiar sight in the hill stations of Peninsular Malaysia growing in exposed areas, and it was commonly cultivated in Singapore. However, it generally prefers a cooler climate. At the foothills of the Himalayas its flowering is spectacular.

Opposite: Spathoglottis plicata was once abundant in open country in Singapore and throughout South-east Asia. It was one of the first plants to re-colonise Krakatoa after the volcanic eruption of 1883 had destroyed all vegetation.

orchid increased as the price dropped, for it came within the means of the average man in the street.

Lester William Bryan visited Singapore in 1920 on an expedition for the Hawaiian Sugar Planters Association and was captivated by the sight of Miss Joaquim blooming luxuriantly at the Botanic Gardens. I.H. Burkill gave him 28 cuttings which he took back to Hilo and propagated. Harold Lyon of the Foster Botanic Gardens in Honolulu accompanied Lester Bryan on one of his trips to Singapore and also took back a few cuttings which formed the nucleus for the Joaquim on Oahu. Interest soon spread to Maui, another sugar-growing area of the Islands. Some of the Joaquim which had been taken to Manila provided a new source of supply for the Hawaiian growers.

A fanciful story is told by Yeoh Bok Choon that initially the Hawaiians did not understand the requirements of Vanda Miss Joaquim and pampered the plants by growing them under shade in a greenhouse. The orchid refused to bloom and after a few seasons the owner pulled out his plants in disgust and threw them out of his greenhouse. Neglected, but now exposed to full sunshine and daily rains, the orchid displayed its full glory. By the mid-1930s, Vanda Miss Joaquim was growing in such profusion in Hawaii that it

A favourite with gardeners and florists the *Dendrobium* is an ideal plant for the novice. The variegated flowers are a rarity in the orchid world. This delightful chimera (*right*) was an accidental spin-off from the cloning process which is now in vogue.

had eclipsed the traditional hibiscus culture of the Islands. "Grown by the acre, sold by the pound, and used by the millions", it was worn by American women at grand openings and commercial events and became the most widely known orchid in the world. In its adopted home, it was often promoted as the Princess Aloha Orchid.

The career of this "Orchid Glamour Girl" was no less spectacular than the performance of a speculative stock on a rising market. Through propagation, William Bryan built up a collection of 10,000 plants before he started to sell the flowers at 35 cents per bloom. Imagine a single stem producing three or four sprays of flowers in bloom at any one time. It was enough to inspire visions of fortune ahead.

During the Joaquim gold rush in Hawaii the big money was made selling cuttings of the plant. As Joaquim roots at every node, cuttings were sold by the feet, a dollar per foot being the standard price. According to Rodney Wilcox Jones, a past president of the American Orchid Society, thousands of people grew Joaquim in Hawaii. Every housewife planted a hedge, and on her way to market cut enough flowers to pay for her groceries.

Despite thousands of cuttings changing hands, the price of Joaquim flowers held initially because the canes were never used for flower production but were instead chopped up to increase the stock of plants. While there were many

Aranda Majulah, a scorpion orchid bred by the Singapore Botanic Gardens.

backyard operations, over a hundred growers were planting Joaquim on a huge scale by the acres. One acre of Vanda Miss Joaquim could hold 250,000 plants. Thus when flower production went into full swing, there was an absolute deluge of flowers and the price dropped from 35 cents per bloom to 1 cent for 100, which was the price Bryan received for the last lot of flowers he sold.

History is interesting to recall but no one ever learns from it, and orchid growers are no exception. In the early 1970s, Singapore saw a flurry of interest in a new orchid called Aranda Christine which rose in price from $25 per foot to $300 per foot. Like Joaquim, Christine was extremely bountiful and could be easily propagated. At that time many farmers, disillusioned by falling pork prices, saw fortunes to be made in orchids and were rushing for the Christines. By 1978 there was such a glut of Christine that the price fell below 50 cents per foot. A decade later the same series of events was repeated with mericloned dendrobiums.

Vanda Miss Joaquim became an important cut flower in Hawaii around 1940. During the Second World War, military personnel passing through the Hawaiian Islands mailed it home as a souvenir, laying the groundwork for its popularity after the War. The mushrooming of airline services after the War brought Vanda Miss Joaquim to the United States where it was readily accepted as a distinct floral novelty. Around 1954, a University of Hawaii survey placed the value of Vanda Miss Joaquim flowers shipped to the United States between 1–1½ million dollars per year. Once an airplane was specifically chartered to carry 4,000 pounds of single flower Joaquim corsages to the United States, and with the corsages averaging 180 flowers to a pound this meant that there were 720,000 Joaquim on the payload. Demand was so great that a production line system was set up by the firm "Orchids of Hawaii"—the flowers were floated in a flume past rows of workers who sorted and graded the flowers, the best grades for corsages, the poorer grades for garlands. A single order for 250,000 Joaquim corsages was "easily handled".

Singapore's export orchid industry was nipped in the bud by the advent of the Second World War. In May 1939 the local newspaper carried a story of an air-freighted parcel containing cut blooms of Vanda Miss Joaquim, *Arachnis hookerana*, and *Arachnis maingayi* which had reached London in a perfect state. The parcel took six days to arrive, a tremendous feat in those days. It was not to be repeated until nearly 20 years later. Unlike Hawaii, Singapore and Malaysia were occupied by the Japanese for four years during the War. It was a tremendous setback for orchid cultivation as private gardens, and even the grass verge along the roads, were turned over to the cultivation of simple food crops like tapioca and sweet potato. Vanda Miss Joaquim and the collection of orchids at the Singapore Botanic Gardens managed to survive because Professor H. Tanakadate, who came out with the Japanese army, allowed Holttum to continue the administration of the Botanic Gardens.

Vanda Miss Joaquim bounced back into prominence after the War because of its great vigour. By 1960 it had become so plentiful that there were complaints in the *Malayan Orchid Review* of a glut of Joaquim flowers in the local market which was causing the price to drop to 12 sticks per dollar.

Times were changing rapidly. Many of the hybrids made before the War were brought to bloom and each often appeared to be better than its predecessor. The bright red Aranthera Anne Black and Aranthera Bloodshot, the yellow Arachnis Maggie Oei, the deep mauve Aranda Wendy Scott, numerous fine *Dendrobiums* and the pride of Singapore, Vanda Tan Chay Yan vied with Vanda Miss Joaquim for centre stage. Because of cheap air freight, local growers had a choice of new hybrids from Hawaii, continental USA and France. Suddenly, everyone was involved in raising new hybrids and the amateur grower stopped growing Vanda Miss Joaquim.

—

In 1981, Singapore came full circle. With the emphasis on landscaping of roads and public gardens, Vanda Miss Joaquim is certain to make a comeback. In style.

Opposite: Arachnis Maggie Oei. This scorpion hybrid is an equal of Vanda Miss Joaquim in toughness, vigour and floriferousness and its flowers are long lasting but they are not as attractive.

In Search of *A Chinese Name*

To the English-speaking public the translation of Vanda Miss Joaquim into Pinyin appeared simple enough. But, in fact, there were different proposals from several interested parties, such as the Chinese-speaking Nanyang Orchid Association, the Orchid Exporters' Association and the Singapore Florist Association.

The problem was that although orchid growing was an ancient art in China, the majority of Chinese scientific names were new. The oldest orchid manual in the world, *The Orchids of King Chang,* published in 1233, described 22 kinds of *Cymbidium* but contemporary experts such as F.H. Wang and S.C. Chen from the Academia Sinica in Beijing are of the opinion that some of the "*Cymbidiums*" probably included other genera like *Calanthe* and *Phaius*. The first attempt by Chinese scientific societies to produce standardised terminologies resulted in a preliminary draft of botanical, zoological and mineralogical terms which contained only 50 Chinese generic names of orchids. This was published by the Scientific Nomenclature Investigation Committee in 1935. The names of 88 additional genera were proposed as recently as 1954. The galaxy of species and hybrid names would be absolutely bewildering if one were to go through the 25,000 species of orchids and an even larger number of man-made hybrids.

Classically, orchids were referred to as **lan** (兰) but this normally meant *Cymbidium virescens* Lindl., the flower which has inspired thousands of Chinese poets and painters. To characterise the different types of orchids, lan was used as a root word and descriptive, legendary or fanciful prefixes were added, e.g. **Chichun lan** (匙唇兰) the "spoon-lip orchid" for *Calypso*; **Shihuo lan** (石活兰) "rock-living orchid" for *Dendrobium* denoting the habitat of a few species peculiar to China (for, in point of fact, *Dendrobium* usually grow on trees, the name being formed from two Greek words, **dendron** which means "tree" and **bios** which means "life" or "living upon"); **Xianren zhijia lan** (仙人指甲兰) Fairy's Fingernail Orchid for *Aerides*, a name derived from legend. *Aerides* has also been referred to as **diao hua**, "hanging flower" by the Jesuit missionary Alvim Semedo in 1613 because the plants were grown suspended from a beam. (In the West, the common name for *Calypso* is Fairy Slipper Orchid and for *Aerides*, the Fox-tail Orchid while *Dendrobium* has no common name.)

Gastrodia elata, whose underground tubers are regarded as an excellent tonic by Chinese herbalists, is a rare parasitic orchid which cannot be found until it sends out its flowering stems. When the stems just emerge from the ground they are called **Chijian** (赤箭), "red arrows". When the inflorescences reach their full height of several feet they are called **Tianma** (天麻), "heavenly hemp". The development of the inflorescence is relatively rapid. Field collectors for herbalists recognise the young shoots and the tall inflorescence, with its numerous, tiny flowers and capsules, to be one and the same plant, so they commonly use the double term **Chijian Tianma**. But in the botanical publications some authors use **Chijian** while others prefer **Tianma**.

Some orchids were not recognised for what they were and they had fanciful Chinese names such as **Yufeng hua** (玉风花) or "jade phoenix flower" for *Habenaria*, **Shan Shanhu** (山珊瑚) or "mountain coral" for *Galeola*, both of which were used for medicinal purposes. On the other hand, some plants which were not members of the orchid family may have the word **lan** incorporated into their names, e.g. **Yu lan** (玉兰) and **Mu lan** (木兰) for Magnolia.

In 1954, T. Tang and F.T. Wang writing in *Acta Phytotaxonomica Sinica* (volume 2, pp. 456–470) proposed 88 new Chinese generic names for orchids, including **Wandailan** (万代兰) for *Vanda*. The techniques they employed to supply the new names included:

1. creating descriptive names, e.g. **Shuo lan** (勺兰) "ladle orchid" for *Cypripedium*. It is interesting to note that the authors have compared the lip of the *Cypripedium* to a ladle for elsewhere it has

always been likened to a slipper (hence the common names Venus Slipper Orchid, Slipper Orchid, **bunga kasut**).

2. translating technical terms from Greek or Latin into Chinese, e.g. **Wuye lan** (无叶兰) or "leafless orchid" for *Aphyllorchis*, a small group of rare saprophytic orchids;

3. translating technical names by sound, e.g. **Wandailan** from the Sanskrit name, *Vanda*;

4. creating names to honour people or places, e.g. **Alishan lan** (啊里山兰) for *Arisanorchis*, which is named after its mountain habitat in central Taiwan; and

5. adopting vernacular names, e.g. **Shidou** (石豆) "rock bean" for *Bulbophyllum* which is a familiar item in the pharmacopoeia of west and south China. The "rock bean" refers to the pseudobulbs of the plants.

This still leaves the problem of denoting the individual species unresolved. For example, while Bulbophyllum is now designated by its vernacular name Shidou, the species which Chinese herbalists use for treating tuberculosis and tumours of the stomach, *Bulbophyllum inconspicuum* is called **Maihu** (麦斛) "small button orchid" because of its tiny pseudobulbs. The herbalists imply *Dendrobium nobile* when they speak of **Shihuo lan** (石活兰) whereas this is now the generic name for *Dendrobium*, one of the largest groupings of orchids

Opposite: Dendrobiums constitute the backbone of the cut flower industry in Singapore, Malaysia and Thailand.

comprising some 900 species.

It should be noted that when Tang and Wang coined a new generic name for an orchid they chose an outstanding character of the genus to create the epithet, and they did not consider it necessary to stay with the original meaning, mythological association or pronunciation of the technical name of Greek, Latin or other language origin. As an extreme example, one could cite the case of the Fairy Slipper Orchid, *Calypso bulbosa*, which is a native of boreal forests across Asia, Europe and North America.

The cool, shaded, mossy habitat and the flower's beauty and rarity have earned for this taiga orchid the name of a goddess from the Odyssey and a reputation among the native peoples of British Columbia as being capable of enhancing the charm of adolescent girls if its bulbs are chewed. In Chinese, it is simply called the "spoon-lip orchid", **Chichun lan** (匙唇兰).

The names proposed for Vanda Miss Joaquim were **Wandai Rujin** (万代如今) which means Everlasting Vanda Orchid, **Rujin Fa lan** (如今发兰) which means Splendid Orchid, and **Zhoujin Wandailan** (卓锦万代兰), a direct transliteration from English. Vanda is normally know as **Wandailan** (万代兰), with **Wandai** meaning "10,000 generations" or "everlasting".

After much discussion, the Ministry of Culture announced on June 14, 1981 that the official Chinese name for Vanda Miss Joaquim was to be **Zhoujin Wandailan** (卓锦万代兰), Orchid of Long-Lasting Excellence.

What is an Orchid, anyway?

*I*n this part of the world, most people immediately form a mental image of a *Vanda*, a scorpion orchid or a *Dendrobium* when they think of an orchid—"straggly plants which, for some reason or other, do not grow on the ground but only in broken brick or charcoal." This image is not quite correct, because many local orchids which were garden favourites in the old days are terrestrial plants like the *Spathoglottis*, *Arundina*, *Bromheadia* and the Slipper Orchids. Their habit of growth also does not mark them as orchids although it serves as a distinguishing point between groups of orchids. Some have a straight, perpendicular growth and are designated as monopodial orchids, while the remainder grow longitudinally by rhizomes (like the ginger plant) and are referred to as sympodial orchids. Vanda Miss Joaquim is a monopodial orchid.

There are tremendous differences in the detailed structure of the flowers of the 25,000 species of orchids, just as there are differences in their ecology. Orchids have been an extremely successful plant form and they have colonised every land mass except Antarctica. In the tropics, many orchids grow perched on the sunny branches of tall trees, but some prefer the lower branches where they only receive dappled sunlight. Others grow on the shady forest floor and a few parasitic orchids even spend their entire life underground, permitting only their flowers to peek above the soil.

The Slipper Orchid of Pulau Langkawi (*Paphiopedilum niveum*) grows on limestone escarpments just above the high tide mark. On Penang Hill, another Slipper Orchid (*Paphiopedilum barbatum*) may be found growing on laterite amid fallen foliage or on moss-covered, granite boulders. Most of our Singapore orchids are epiphytes which grow on trees, the pigeon orchid (*Dendrobium crumenatum*) being the commonest. Orchids can also be found at the edge of the desert and in the Arctic. Nearly all orchids are adapted to water stress. Their roots have a cork-like covering called **velamen** which leaves bare only the absorbent tips of the roots. In Vanda Miss Joaquim, the stems and the thick, pencil-shaped leaves are also modified water storage organs.

DISTINGUISHING FEATURES

All orchid flowers have a few features in common which distinguish them from other flowering plants. The orchid flower has three sepals and three petals. One of the petals is intricately shaped and is more colourful than the rest of the flower. This is the **lip,** which acts as a landing platform for insects, an ingenious adaptation designed to ensure pollination. The patterns on the lip in Vanda Miss Joaquim and its parents (best seen in ultraviolet light) serve as nectar guides for the bees causing them to move in a specific direction and manner once it lands

Opposite: The giant orchid *Grammatophyllum speciosum*, a Singapore native, is the largest orchid in the world.

on the flower so that it transfers pollen from flower to flower. Above the lip, and partially hidden by it is the column, a structure formed by the fusion of the male (**stamen**) and the female (**pistil**) parts of the flower. This column is the hallmark of the orchid. In Vanda Miss Joaquim the column is topped by an **anther cap** which covers the two yellow masses of pollinia. Below this is a sticky concave pit which is the **stigma** of the flower.

The lip of Vanda Miss Joaquim has a curious pouch called the **spur** which points downwards and backwards in the open flower. In the young buds atop the inflorescence the spurs point upwards. As the buds mature, the "stem" of the flower (in point of fact, it is the **ovary**) twists through 180 degrees so that the lip and spur point downwards in the open flower. This twist is common to many orchids but it is by no means universal.

TOWARDS SURVIVAL

The varied, sometimes even bizarre, shapes assumed by orchid flowers are adaptations to ensure pollination. Three years after he published *The Origin of Species*, Charles Darwin came out with a book entitled *On the Various Contrivances by which Orchids are Fertilised by Insects* in which he stated that the contrivances "are as varied and almost as perfect as the most beautiful adaptations in the animal kingdom".

Above: The vivid markings on the lip of *Vanda teres* variety Andersoni serve as nectar guides to large carpenter bees which pollinate the flower.

Opposite: Aranthera Beatrice Ng variety Conference Gold. The golden colour is uncommon in the orchid world and a rarity in the scorpion orchids.

Orchids mimic insects or their prey, shoot pollen at the insects as they depart from the flower, set traps to capture insects, which must then crawl through exit tunnels past pollen masses to escape from drowning, or provide deep wells of sweet nectar so that only those night flying moths endowed with a 30 cm tongue can drink from them and pollinate the flowers. When all else fails, some orchids self-pollinate. The "ladies' tassels" (*Spiranthes sinensis*) which were described some 3,000 years ago in the Chinese *Book of Poetry* have a distribution which extends all the way from Siberia through China, Indo-China and Malaysia to Australia and New Zealand. In its northern habitats the flower opens widely and is insect-pollinated, but as the species progresses southwards, the flowers tend to be closed and tubular and in New Zealand they are self-pollinating.

A seed capsule develops after the orchid flower is pollinated. It may take a couple of weeks to mature in some species and up to a year in others. In the capsule, thousands of microscopic seeds develop. They are released into the wind when the capsule dehisces and may be blown for miles before they settle on land. Each seed must find the special fungus, the mycorrhiza, which will provide it with sugar during the early stages of its germination for in its total adaptation for wind dispersal the orchid seed has given up all its food stores. In spite of this precarious relationship the orchid has managed to survive and become the largest family of flowering plants in the world.

How to Grow
The National Flower

To recapitulate, Vanda Miss Joaquim requires full sunlight, free air movement, high humidity and heavy fertilising to achieve optimum growth and flowering. It needs support to grow straight and tall, but it flowers only when the top 40–50 cm of its stem rises above the support. It is a robust plant which branches freely and soon becomes a dense clump. Therefore, it is best grown in beds on the ground. It may be tied to vertical posts of 100 cm in height or it may be supported by slim horizontal beams which can be added as the plants grow taller, thereby not impeding flowering.

In the olden days vertical pillars were preferred because the most practical way of providing a continuous supply of nutrients was to slap cattle manure on to the posts around the roots. The poles, 6 cm in diameter and 100 cm in length, are staked about 50 cm apart in a shallow trench 20 cm deep.

A layer of crock and broken bricks is laid to a depth of 15 cm to allow for free drainage and aeration around the roots. Six to eight cuttings of 60–70 cm in height are tied around the pole and the plants are watered twice a day until new roots appear. At this stage wet cattle manure is plastered around the plants to a height of 40 cm and gradually the whole bed is filled with manure to a depth of 15 cm. To reduce evaporation, the beds are covered with lawn grass or compost.

Chemical fertilisers are more acceptable today and in non-commercial gardens the organic fertilisers are generally restricted to bone meal and sludge, either of which can be added to the feeding roots at the base of the plants. Garden compost, cut grass, lallang or wood shavings must be placed around the base to a height of 15 cm. In the Philippines, **Ipil-lpil** (*Leucaenia glauca*) stems are planted around the base for support of the roots. It is helpful, though not absolutely necessary, to shade the plants for a few weeks until the new roots are established. The plants should be watered two to three times a day. Tan Hoon Siang reported in 1963 that by watering three to four times a day with cow manure in the mulch, he could produce sprays carrying 15 flowers. Furthermore, if the plants are grown up to three metres, the number of flowers per spray will increase. However, if water is not given at least three times a day, the sprays will be shorter and the flowers fewer in number.

Vanda Miss Joaquim is relatively free from disease and pests apart from red spiders which attack the entire plant, and aphids and beetles which feed on the flowers. These can be controlled by periodic spraying with Malathion and other insecticides. Red spider predators are now available in England and could be beneficially introduced in Singapore.

The size of the plant, its freshness and turgidity, its ability to remain green from the base to the top are indications whether the plant has been given the right growing conditions. Additionally, it should flower continuously with a peak flowering between February and June. When really well grown, each plant should carry two or three inflorescences at a time, each with 12 flowers 5–6 cm across.

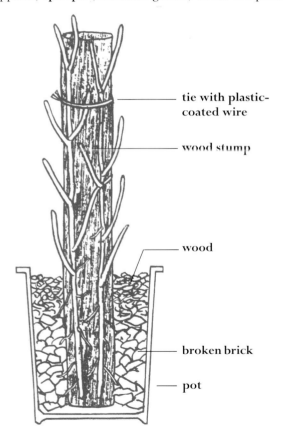

tie with plastic-coated wire

wood stump

wood

broken brick

pot

Opposite: Landscape planting of Vanda Miss Joaquim at the Singapore Botanic Gardens.

The Hybrids of
Vanda Miss Joaquim

he creation and nurturing of an orchid hybrid to maturity is an irresistible adventure for an orchid grower. It takes years for a hybrid to bloom, and even the most experienced grower still looks with fond anticipation to its first flowering. Every gardener wants to have a wide range of orchids flowering in his garden, of different shapes, sizes and colour, and many are perpetually looking out for novelties. Experience has shown that although orchids which are accustomed to marked seasonal changes or to a cooler climate do not flower well, and sometimes not at all in Singapore, hybrids with a local species often present no problem. Vanda Miss Joaquim has been incorporated into hundreds of different hybrids in the hope that it will impart certain desirable qualities, such as the ability to flower throughout the year, clear colour and resilience.

To a large extent these objectives have been achieved. The choice of crosses is restricted to what hybridisers have in their collections. In the beginning, the only plants available in Singapore were the parental species, *Vanda hookerana* and *Vanda teres*; and more showy species like *Vanda dearei*, *Vanda luzonica*, *Vanda sanderana*, *Vanda spathulata* and *Vanda tricolor*. These were all bred with Vanda Miss Joaquim.

The backcross to *Vanda hookerana* produced Vanda Cooperi which was very similar in shape and colouring to its *hookerana* parent but it was larger and more robust, though not quite as free flowering as Vanda Miss Joaquim. A unique strain called variety "White Wings" (a cross between Vanda Miss Joaquim var. Josephine, and *Vanda hookerana* alba) was subsequently crossed with an alba *Vanda teres* to produce Vanda Diana, a white Vanda similar in shape to Vanda Miss Joaquim. The similarity of the two hybrids was due to the fact that both had only *Vanda hookerana* and *Vanda teres* in their parentage; 50:50 in the case of Vanda Miss Joaquim and 37.5 percent *hookerana* and 62.5 percent *teres* in Vanda Diana. Vanda Diana is a robust plant, quite free flowering and very popular with local growers. Unfortunately, the intervention of the Second World War prevented Singapore from registering the hybrid with the Royal Horticultural Society in London so the Hawaiians have precedence with the name: the hybrid is now properly called Vanda Poepoe variety Diana.

The backcross to *Vanda teres* was done in Java and it produced a fertile, pink hybrid named Vanda Miss van Deun. Further crossing produced such interesting free flowering hybrids as Vanda Petamboeran and Vanda Marlie Dolera (Vanda Petamboeran x *Vanda sanderana*). Another lovely, early Javanese hybrid is the blue Vanda Prinses Beatrix, a cross between Vanda Miss Joaquim and the blue *Vanda coerulea* which hails from the cool

Opposite: The beautiful, large, flat flowers of Vanda Marlie Dolera are the result of a complex crossing from Vanda Miss Joaquim which included the large Philippine *Vanda sanderana* in the final step. (F3 hybrid)

Left: A crossing between Vanda Miss Joaquim and the colourful, variable, Indonesian *Vanda tricolor* produced many distinct varieties of Vanda E.M.E. Dinger. *Above:* Variety Audrey. (Water colour paintings from the Herbarium, courtesy of the Singapore Botanic Gardens).

Following pages: (*Left*) Vanda Miss Joaquim variety Douglas, a giant colourful tetraploid clone produced in Hawaii for hybridisation purposes. (*Right*) Miniaturisation is a popular goal in modern hybridisation, achieved in this hybrid by crossing with ascocenda.

Sooner or later, every orchid is crossed with the colossal Philippine strap-leafed **Waling-waling** (Tagalog for "beautiful"), *Vanda sanderana*. Vanda Merv. L. Velthius (Vanda Miss Joaquim x *Vanda sanderana*) has the size and colouring of *Vanda sanderana* and the floriferousness, vigour and sunlight tolerance of Vanda Miss Joaquim.

Sometimes, one parent completely overshadows the other because it contributes twice or three times the amount of genetic material. Such was the case with Vanda Cobber Kain because the yellow *Vanda spathulata* from Sri Lanka was hexaploid (it has six sets of chromosomes). Its tertiary hybrid, Vanda Candlelight (Vanda Cobber Kain x *Vanda sanderana*) is also completely dominated by *Vanda spathulata* and the influence of Vanda Miss Joaquim is barely noticeable.

As the years passed, the orchidists became more sophisticated and line breeding was pursued to obtain certain colours. Vanda Poepoe var. Diana produced a large, immaculate, white Vanda Lily Wong when it was bred with an alba *Vanda sanderana*: next, it was crossed with Vanda Hilo Blue and this produced the blue-mauve Vanda Kenny Kwek.

Miniaturisation also became important as garden space has decreased. The genus *Ascocentrum*, a group of "miniature Vanda" from Thailand, revealed its tremendous potential when its first hybrids with Vanda produced spectacular sprays of flat, round, colourful flowers on dwarf

mountainous regions of northwestern Thailand, northern Burma and India. While it is very difficult to maintain *Vanda coerulea* in a good state in the lowlands, let alone flower it, Vanda Prinses Beatrix flourishes in full sunlight and is fairly free flowering.

plants. With Vanda Miss Joaquim, the influx of *Ascocentrum* blood has produced many delightful crosses, amongst the 46 such hybrids registered by 1997.

At the end of 1996, or slightly more than a century after its debut, Vanda Miss Joaquim has been bred into 440 hybrids. Among Vandas, it was one of the Top Ten Parents up to 1990, rubbing shoulders with *Vanda sanderana, Vanda coerulea*, Vanda Rothschildiana and Vanda Josephine van Brero. As a hybrid Vanda, it was the fourth most popular parent.

Singapore, Malaysian and Hawaiian hybridisers have been actively extending the family tree of Vanda Miss Joaquim in an effort to produce, in a full range of colours, large, flat, round Vandas (taking *Vanda sanderana* as the gold standard) that can withstand full sunlight, heavy rains, and flower year round (with Vanda Miss Joaquim as the gold standard). Only some of these goals have been achieved, but there are already 177 second generation, 119 third generation, 43 fourth generation and 13 fifth generation progeny.

Opposite: This hybrid of Vanda Miss Joaquim with *Paraphalaenopsis laycockii* flowers on a perpetually diminutive plant.

Left: Vanda Rothschildiana, the ever-popular primary hybrid between *Vanda sanderana* and *Vanda coerulea*.

Following pages, left: (*Top*) An advanced *Vanda sanderana* hybrid demonstrating desirable floral shape imparted by *Vanda sanderana*. (*Bottom left*) Vanda Penang Manila (F2 hybrid of Joaquim). (*Bottom right*) Vanda Merv. L. Velthius (F1 hybrid of Joaquim).

Following pages, right: This F3 hybrid produced a wide range of colour forms.

Corsages, Buttonholes, Leis and Arrangements

The flowers of Vanda Miss Joaquim are ideal for buttonholes, corsages, bouquets, leis and flower arrangements. The removal of all the flowering sprays from a single orchid plant actually stimulates the development of the next crop of flowers, so if you grow your own Joaquim, you should not hesitate to cut the flowers from time to time and try using them in various ways. The sprays should be cut when they have reached their peak of perfection: in the case of Joaquim, this is when the third flower on the stem is two days open and has reached its deepest hue. Only cut those flowers that are without blemish and take care not to knock off the pollen or anther cap when you handle the flower. If the pollen is removed, the flower fades within a few hours and gives off ethylene gas. In an enclosed space, e.g. a box or refrigerator, this causes all the flowers around it to fade. To season the flowers make a fresh oblique cut on the stem underwater and leave to soak for a few hours.

If the blooms are to be used for buttonholes, bouquets and garlands, they may be removed singly. Again, only select the mature, perfect flower at its peak. The flowers are placed in a tray of water until the petals are turgid. With orchids, you can harvest the flowers at any time of the day. After seasoning, the flowers can be left in a polythene bag in the refrigerator overnight if necessary.

HOW TO MAKE A CORSAGE

1. Select the most perfect blooms and season for 4–5 hours, or preferably overnight.
2. The stems of individual flowers need to be reinforced with a thin silver wire. This can be used to lengthen the stem and it also makes it more pliable for positioning. Make a small loop on the silver wire and pass the long end through the column of the flower, then twist around the stem.
3. To prolong the life of the flower, add a small wad of wet cotton wool and if the stem needs lengthening a stiffer piece of wire can be added.
4. Wrap dark green florist tape around the stem beyond the cotton wool.

5. Arrange the flowers and foliage together and carefully twist florist tape around the stems to hold the arrangement in place.
6. If you wish, tie a ribbon or bow.
7. The corsage may be stored in the refrigerator for a day. If you intend to store longer, wrap with cellophane or place in a box before keeping in the refrigerator.

HOW TO MAKE A LEI (GARLAND)

1. Pluck off individual flowers and season them by soaking in water for 2–4 hours.
2. Use transparent nylon for threading as this will give a better hold and is less likely to damage the flowers.
3. In a lei, the flowers are held horizontally across the axis of the lei and each flower should be threaded through the lateral (lower) sepals and the base of the lip (see diagram).
4. Arrange the flowers into a helix.
5. Second grade flowers may be used for leis.

Opposite: (Left) For many women, like the author's wife, the orchid lei brings fond memories of Hawaii. *(Right)* Vanda Miss Joaquim made into a bridal bouquet (Courtesy of Michael Ong of Fleuridee Florist).

Glossary

Common Name	Botanical Name	Common Name	Botanical Name
Alishan lan	*Arisanorchis*	**Shidou**	*Bulbophyllum*
Black orchid	*Coelogyne pandurata*	**Shihuo lan**	*Dendrobium*
Carpenter bee	*Xylocopa sp.*	**Shuo lan**	*Cypripedium*
Chichun lan	*Calypso*	Slipper orchid on Penang Hill	*Paphiopedilum barbatum*
Cooktown orchid	*Dendrobium phalaenopsis*	Slipper orchid of Pulau Langkawi	*Paphiopedilum niveum*
Flor de San Sebastian	*Cattleya skinneri*		
Giant orchid	*Grammatophyllum speciosum*	Stone orchid	*Dendrobium moniliforme*
Ipil-ipil	*Leucaenia glauca*	Tassel grass or ladies' tassels	*Spiranthes sinensis*
Jewel orchid	*Macodes petola*	**Tianma** (at full height)	*Gastrodia elata*
Kinta weed	*Vanda hookerana*	**Waling-waling**	*Vanda sanderana*
Maihu	*Bulbophyllum inconspicuum*	White moth orchid (**anggrek bulan** in Indonesia)	*Phalaenopsis amabilis*
Moccasin Orchid	*Cypripedium reginae*		
Monja Blanca	*Lycaste virginalis*	White scorpion orchid	*Arachnis hookerana*
Moth orchid	*Phalaenopsis*	Wind orchid	*Neofinetia falcata*
Pigeon orchid	*Dendrobium crumenatum*	**Wuye lan**	*Aphyllorchis*
Sampaguita	*Jasminum sambac*	**Xianren zhijia lan**	*Aerides*
Shan shanhu	*Galeola*	**Yufeng hua**	*Habenaria*
		Zijian (emerging)	*Gastrodia elata*

Acknowledgements

I have drawn on various sources to obtain material for this book and would like to thank:

Mrs Ng Siew Yin, the Assistant Commissioner, Singapore Botanic Gardens, for permission to photograph and reproduce several orchid paintings from the Herbarium collection;

The Director, Royal Botanic Gardens at Kew for permission to reproduce three old paintings from the *Curtis Botanical Review*;

The Osaka Municipal Museum for the photograph of the brush painting of uprooted orchids by Cheng Ssu-hsiao;

Mr Arshak Galstaun for information on the Joaquim family and the photograph of Regina Joaquim with her husband;

Mr Quek Kiah Huat for the loan of the painting of *Orchids and Bamboo;*

Mr Michael Ong of Fleuridee for making the bridal bouquet with Vanda Miss Joaquim;

Mdm Yew Soo Teen of Greenleaf Florist for making the corsage;

And my orchid friends who have made it possible for me to make a photographic study of Vanda Miss Joaquim and other orchids.

References

ALPHONSO, A.G. "Singapore's National Flower (Vanda Miss Joaquim)", *Malayan Orchid Review,* 15: 9, 1981.

ANONYMOUS *A Barefoot Doctor's Manual* (translated from the Chinese). Philadelphia: Rising Press, 1977.

BOWIE., H.P. *On the Laws of Japanese Painting* New York: Dover Publications, 1952.

BURKILL. H.M. "The Role of the Singapore Botanic Gardens in the Development of Orchid Hybrids." Proceedings of the 4th World Orchid Conference, 1963, p. 10. Singapore: Straits Times Press.

BURKHILL, I.H. & MOHAMED HANIFF. "Malay Village Medicine". The Gardener's Bulletin, Straits Settlement, Vol VI, Part 2, 1930.

DEWOLF, G.P. JR. "Vanda Miss Joaquim in Hawaii", *American Orchid Society Bulletin*, 22: 724, 1953.

GALISTAN, E. "Cultural Notes on Garden Orchids", *Malayan Orchid Review*, 1: 21, 1931.

HENDERSON M.R. & ADDISON, G. *Malayan Orchid Hybrids*. Singapore: Government Printing Office, 1957.

HOLTTUM, R.E. Editorial, Malayan Orchid Review. 1(2): 1, 1932.

HOLTTUM, R.E. "Singapore Hybrids", *M.O.R.* 2: 147, 1938.

HOLTTUM, R.E. "Four New Vanda Hybrids", *M.O.R.* 3: 10, 1940 .

HOLTTUM, R.E. "Recent Hybrids Raised in Singapore", *M.O.R.*, 1949.

HOLTTUM, R.E. *A Revised Flora of Malaya* Vol. 1, Orchids, 3rd ed. Singapore: Government Printing Office, 1964.

HU, S.Y. "Whence the Chinese Generic Names of Orchids", *American Orchid Society Bulletin* 34: 519, 1965.

JONES, R.W. "Vanda Miss Joaquim, Orchid Glamour Girl", *American Orchid Society Bulletin*, 29: 687, 1960.

KOAY, S.M. "The Singapore Orchid Industry—Challenges and Prospects" Malayan Orchid Review 29: 84, 1995.

LAYCOCK, J. "Picture of a Singapore Collection (1949 A.D.) *Malayan Orchid Review* 4: 3,]949.

LAYCOCK, J. "Vanda Miss Joaquim", *Philippine Orchid Review*, 11: 3, 1949.

LEE, K.H. & EDE, J. "Cut Flowers for Export", *Malayan Orchid Review*, 6: 16, 1961.

MALAYAN ORCHID REVIEW. Editorial, 1: 1, 1931.

MALAYAN ORCHID REVIEW. "Notes on Orchid Prices in Singapore", 1: 27, 1931.

NEW NATION. "Flower for All", March 19, 1981.

QUISUMBING. E. "Vandas of the Philippines" *Philippine Orchid Review*, 1949.

RIDLEY, N. H. "New and Noteworthy Plants", *The Gardener's Chronicle* p. 740, 1893.

ROYAL HORTICULTURAL SOCIETY. The RHS Orchid Registration CD 1997.

SCHULTES, R.E. & PEASE, A.S. *Generic Names of Orchids: Their Origin and Meaning*. London: Academic Press, 1963.

STEPHENS, J.A. "Vanda Miss Joaquim", American Orchid Society Bulletin 23: 366, 1954.

STRAITS TIMES. "National Flower Week Will Bloom in July", March 20, 1981.

STRAITS TIMES. "Vanda Miss Joaquim—The Popular Choice", April 16, 1981.

STRAITS TIMES. "National Flower is an Elusive Lady", May 11, 1981.

STRAITS TIMES. "Call to Grow National Flower in Community Centres and Schools", May 12, 1981.

STRAITS TIMES. "How About Wandai Roujin Says Assn.", June 2, 1981.

STRAITS TIMES. "Gardens to Mass Produce National Flower", July 31, 1981.

SULLIVAN, M. The *Three Perfections: Chinese Painting, Poetry and Calligraphy*. London: Thames and Hudson, 1974.

SUNDAY NATION. "Her Tombstone Found—New Light Shed on Miss Joaquim", July 19, 1981.

SUNDAY TIMES. "National Flower, And Now the Official Chinese Name", June 14, 1981.

TAN, H.S. "The Culture of Vandaceous Plants in Malaya", Proceedings of the 4th World Orchid Conference. Singapore: Straits Times Press, p. 85, 1963.

TANG, T. & WANG F.T. "Orchidaeceae: Keys to the Subfamilies, Divisions, Tribes, Series, Subseries, Subtribes and Genera." *Acta Phytotaxonomica Sinica*, 2: 456, 1954.

TEOH, F.S. *Orchids*. Singapore: Orchid Society of South-East Asia, 1978.

TEOH, E.S. *Asian Orchids*. Singapore: Times Books International, 1980.

TEOH, E.S. "Viewpoint: Vanda Miss Joaquim, National Flower of Singapore", *Malayan Orchid Review*, 15: 5, 1981.

WANG, F.H. & CHEN, S.C. "Orchids of China" in Lawler, L. & Kerr, R.D. (eds.), *Proceedings of the Orchid Symposium*. Sydney: Orchid Society of New South Wales, 1981.

YEOH, B.C. "Kinta Weed", *Malayan Orchid Review*, 5: 81, 1959.

YEOH, B.C. "Miss Joaquim's Orchid", M.O.R., 7(2): 36, 1963.